STUDY GUIDE

The Great Commission

Burk Parsons

LIGONIER MINISTRIES
Renew your Mind.
LIGONIER.ORG | 800-435-4343

421 Ligonier Court, Sanford, FL 32771
E-mail: info@ligonier.org

Printed in China.

Contents

Introduction

From Genesis to Revelation, the mission of God is focused on God saving a people for Himself from every tribe, tongue, and nation. Our Lord Jesus Christ gave His people the Great Commission to make disciples of all nations. This is a significant task, yet it is one that the Holy Spirit enables His church to accomplish as we rest in the authority of Christ over all things. In this series, Dr. Burk Parsons walks us through every phrase of the Great Commission, carefully examining how Christ calls us to fulfill the Great Commission by God's sovereign power, according to His appointed means, and for His glory alone.

This study guide is a companion to the video teaching series. Whether you are using the DVDs, streaming the videos on Ligonier.org, or going through the course in Ligonier Connect, this resource is designed to help you make the most of the learning experience. For each message in the series, there is a corresponding lesson in this guide. Here is what you will find in each lesson:

INTRODUCTION	The introduction is a brief paragraph that summarizes the content covered in the lecture and considered in the study guide lesson. **How to use:** Use the introduction to each lesson to get a sense of the big picture before watching the video. Refer to these statements as you work through the study guide to remind yourself of what have already covered and where you are headed.
LEARNING GOALS	The learning goals are the knowledge and skills with which the study guide lesson will endeavor to equip you as you work through the lecture content. **How to use:** Familiarize yourself with the goals of each lesson before engaging with its contents. Keeping the overall purpose in mind as you watch each video and reflect on or discuss the questions will help you get the most out of each lesson.

KEY IDEAS	The key ideas are the major points or takeaways from the lecture. **How to use:** Use these ideas to prepare yourself for each lesson and to review previous lessons. They describe specifically the knowledge each lecture is communicating.
REFLECTION & DISCUSSION QUESTIONS	The questions are the guided reflection and discussion component of the lesson that are intended to help you prepare for, process, and organize what you are learning. **How to use:** Reflect on individually or discuss in a group the questions in the order in which they appear in the lesson. The ▶ icon indicates where to play and to pause the video for questions that address specific segments of the lecture.
PRAYER	The prayer section offers suggestions for how to close the lesson in prayer with respect to what was taught in the lecture. **How to use:** Consider using each lesson's prayer section as a guide to personal or group prayer. These sections follow the ACTS prayer model, about which you can learn more in R.C. Sproul's Crucial Questions booklet *Does Prayer Change Things?* This helpful guide is available as a free e-book at Ligonier.org.
REVIEW QUIZ	The review quiz is a set of six multiple-choice questions that appears at the end of each lesson. **How to use:** Use each quiz to check your comprehension and memory of the major points covered in each lecture. It will be most beneficial to your learning if you take a lesson's quiz either sometime between lessons or just before you begin the next lesson in the study guide.
ANSWER KEY	The answer key provides explanations for the reflection and discussion questions and answers to the multiple-choice questions in the review quiz. **How to use:** Use the answer key to check your own answers or when you do not know the answer. Note: Do not give in too quickly; struggling for a few moments to recall an answer reinforces it in your mind.

1

They Worshiped Him

INTRODUCTION

The Great Commission is given in the context of worship. When Jesus' followers encountered Him after the resurrection, they fell down and worshiped Him, and He commissioned them to fulfill His mission in making disciples and taking the gospel to the ends of the earth. In this lesson, Dr. Parsons introduces the Great Commission by looking at the reason why God created us: that He might be worshiped.

LEARNING GOALS

When you have finished this lesson, you should be able to:

- Describe the overall setting of the Great Commission in the book of Matthew
- Identify the central theme of worship within the context of the Great Commission

KEY IDEAS

- The Great Commission is one of the most foundational commands in all of Scripture.
- Worship is the fulfillment of the mission of God, because God created us for worship.
- The Great Commission is given within the context of worship: the disciples of Jesus worshiped at His feet and were sent so that others might worship Him.

REFLECTION & DISCUSSION QUESTIONS

Before the Video

What Do You Think?

- Why do we exist? Why did God choose to create us?

- What feelings do you have when confronted with the overall scope and weightiness of the Great Commission? Is obedience to the Great Commission required of some Christians only or is it required of all Christians? Why?

Scripture Reading

> *All authority in heaven and on earth has been given to me. Go therefore and make disciples of all nations, baptizing them in the name of the Father and of the Son and of the Holy Spirit, teaching them to observe all that I have commanded you. And I am with you always, to the end of the age.*
>
> —Matthew 28:18b–20

- What are the different commands found within the Great Commission?

During the Video

Play the video; pause at 7:12.

Setting the Scene

- What is the overall setting of the Great Commission? Consider not only the location but also the timeline in the life of Christ and to whom it was given.
- What type of events typically occur on mountains throughout the Bible and particularly in the gospel of Matthew? What are some examples of these types of events?

Play the video; pause at 14:34.

The Purpose of Life

- What did the disciples do when they saw Jesus before receiving the Great Commission?
- Why did God create us? Did He need to create us? Why or why not?
- How does God's reason for creating us inform how we are to relate to creation?

After the Video

- The Bible does not use the name "the Great Commission" in reference to the commands that Jesus gave to His disciples in Matthew 28. Why are these commands traditionally referred to as "the Great Commission"? In what way might the name "the Great Commission" be misleading?

  If you are in a group, have the members discuss how the Great Commission makes them feel. Does it make them feel passionate about the spread of the gospel? Or does it make them feel guilt and shame? Why?

- What does the reaction of the disciples upon seeing Jesus after His resurrection tell us about what the disciples thought of themselves and what they thought of Jesus?

If you are in a group, have the members name various ways in which we can worship God. Are any of these ways more significant than others?

- Some of the disciples experienced an internal conflict and doubted when they saw Jesus after His resurrection. How does the fact that this is recorded in the New Testament provide an argument for the infallibility of the Bible?

  If you are in a group, have each member say whether they consider the doubt of the disciples to be an encouragement or discouragement and explain why. In addition, have each member identify one or two heroes of the faith who also serve as an argument for the veracity of the Bible.

PRAYER

- Praise God for creating us to find our purpose in worship.
- Confess the areas where you are prone to worship creation rather than the Creator.
- Thank God for making you a part of His mission to make worshipers of all people.
- Ask God to equip and empower you as an instrument in fulfilling the Great Commission.

REVIEW QUIZ

1. What region did Jesus tell the women to send the disciples to after His resurrection?
   a. Tyre
   b. Judea
   c. Galilee
   d. Samaria

2. What geographical feature is the locale for many of the redemptive-historical events in the book of Matthew?
   a. Rivers
   b. Deserts
   c. Valleys
   d. Mountains

3. What word best describes what the Great Commission ought to be?
   a. Easy
   b. Difficult
   c. Ordinary
   d. Extraordinary

4. Of the following disciples, who is the most likely to have doubted when seeing Jesus?
   a. John
   b. Judas
   c. Andrew
   d. Matthew
5. Obedience to the Great Commission will involve sacrifice to one degree or another.
   a. True
   b. False
6. What is another nuance of the verb describing the disciples' doubt when they saw Jesus?
   a. Dread
   b. Disbelief
   c. Hesitation
   d. Confusion

Answer Key—They Worshiped Him

REFLECTION & DISCUSSION QUESTIONS

◷ Before the Video

What Do You Think?

These are personal questions. The answers should be based on your own knowledge and experience.

Scripture Reading

- What are the different commands found within the Great Commission?

  Four distinct commands are found within the Great Commission. The first two commands are primary commands. We are commanded to "go" and "make disciples." The second two commands describe the nature of how disciples are to be made, by "baptizing them" and by "teaching them to observe" everything that Jesus has commanded us.

◷ *During the Video*

Setting the Scene

- What is the overall setting of the Great Commission? Consider not only the location but also the timeline in the life of Christ and to whom it was given.

  Jesus gave the Great Commission to the eleven disciples on a mountain in Galilee after his resurrection. The details of this scene can be found in Matthew 28:16, as well as in Matthew 28:7–10, as referenced by Dr. Parsons.

- What type of events typically occur on mountains throughout the Bible and particularly in the gospel of Matthew? What are some examples of these types of events?

  Mountains are often the scene of significant redemptive-historical events throughout the Bible and in the gospel of Matthew. Mountains are often the places where God discloses Himself, revealing who He is and His will for His people. In the Old Testament and in Matthew, some examples of redemptive-historical events that take place on mountains include the revelation of the law on Mount Sinai, the Sermon on the Mount, and the transfiguration.

The Purpose of Life

- What did the disciples do when they saw Jesus before receiving the Great Commission?

  Quite simply, the disciples worshiped Him. We do not know all the details of how this looked but it is likely that the disciples were on their knees or prostrate before

Him in reverence and awe. Strikingly, we are also told that, even in the midst of such worship, some of the disciples doubted (Matt. 28:17).

- Why did God create us? Did He need to create us? Why or why not?

  God created us for worship. The Westminster Shorter Catechism states that "man's chief end is to glorify God and enjoy him forever." We glorify God by worshiping Him, and thus we fulfill the purpose for which we were created. God did not need to create us, because He is perfect and complete in all His attributes and eternal and self-sufficient. The encouraging thing is that He wanted to create us, that we might be His people in worship.

- How does God's reason for creating us inform how we are to relate to creation?

  God created us to worship Him, which informs us of how we are to relate to creation as something that is fundamentally not to be worshiped. We worship the Creator and not the creation. This entails being good stewards of God's creation for the sake of His mission, that the gospel would reach to the ends of the earth and to future generations.

After the Video

- The Bible does not use the name "the Great Commission" in reference to the commands that Jesus gave to His disciples in Matthew 28. Why are these commands traditionally referred to as "the Great Commission"? In what way might the name "the Great Commission" be misleading?

  While the Bible does not use the name, the commands that Jesus gave to His disciples in Matthew 28 have traditionally been called "the Great Commission." This name is appropriate when we consider the significance, scope, and weightiness of what the Great Commission calls us to do. Nonetheless, this name may be misleading if we fail to recognize that the Great Commission is an ordinary calling for every Christian. Obedience to it ought to be the general practice of all Christians.

- What does the reaction of the disciples upon seeing Jesus after His resurrection tell us about what the disciples thought of themselves and what they thought of Jesus?

  When the disciples saw Jesus Christ after His resurrection, they worshiped Him. This tells us that the disciples understood that they were encountering nothing short of the Lord God Almighty, in all His holiness. The disciples reacted with fear and trembling, recognizing their unholiness and need for a righteous and holy God and Savior. Reactions like this are typical throughout the Bible for all those who encounter God in reverence.

- Some of the disciples experienced an internal conflict and doubted when they saw Jesus after His resurrection. How does the fact that this is recorded in the New Testament provide an argument for the infallibility of the Bible?

  The fact that the shortcomings of the disciples are recorded in the Bible provides a strong argument for the infallibility of the Bible, because it shows that the record of the life of Jesus Christ isn't a fabrication. As a piece of historically accurate literature, the Bible even describes the failures and weaknesses of the closest followers of Jesus Christ.

REVIEW QUIZ

1. **C.**
   In Matthew 28:16, we see that the disciples went to Galilee to meet Jesus, who had told the women who first witnessed the resurrection to send His disciples there in Matthew 28:10.
2. **D.**
   Mountains are important redemptive-historical locales throughout the Bible and in the gospel of Matthew. In the gospel of Matthew, such redemptive-historical events include the Sermon on the Mount, the transfiguration, and the Great Commission.
3. **C.**
   While traditionally called "the Great Commission" because of its worldwide scope, the word "ordinary" best describes what the Great Commission ought to be. Christ has called us to ordinary obedience in the Great Commission, and it should be the general practice of every Christian and every church in fulfilling the mission of God.
4. **D.**
   Dr. Parsons suggested a few possibilities to answer this question: possibly Thomas, who we know doubted Jesus, or possibly Peter, who we know denied Jesus. Dr. Parsons also conjectured that Matthew was likely to have doubted, being the author of this book of the Bible and knowing his own heart.
5. **A.**
   Obedience to the Great Commission will certainly involve sacrifice over comfort, as we strive to be obedient by giving up our time, treasures, and talents for the sake of God's mission to the nations.
6. **C.**
   The Greek word used for the internal conflict of the disciples when first seeing the resurrected Christ is translated as "doubted" in the English Standard Version. Also, within the semantic range of this word is the idea of hesitation. Perhaps the disciples hesitated in acknowledging and recognizing Jesus in His resurrected body.

2

All Authority in Heaven and on Earth

INTRODUCTION

The first words of the Great Commission reveal that Jesus Christ has been given all authority in heaven and on the earth, and it is by this authority that we are sent into every corner of the earth, confident that Christ's rule extends over every nation. In this lesson, Dr. Parsons explains how the sovereignty of Jesus Christ is one of the greatest motivations for missions and our greatest assurance of success.

LEARNING GOALS

When you have finished this lesson, you should be able to:

- Name the primary motivations for fulfilling the Great Commission
- Understand the relationship between God's sovereignty and missions

KEY IDEAS

- The first words of the Great Commission are words of reassurance.
- The foundation of the Great Commission is the sovereignty of Jesus Christ.
- The sovereignty of God in salvation makes evangelism and missions possible.

REFLECTION & DISCUSSION QUESTIONS

Before the Video

What Do You Think?

- Do you love God? Do you love your neighbor as yourself? How do you succeed and/or fail in fulfilling these commands?
- What should be some of our primary motives for taking part in the mission of God?

- How have you struggled to understand the relationship between God's sovereignty and man's responsibility in things such as prayer and evangelism?

Scripture Reading

> *I saw in the night visions, and behold, with the clouds of heaven there came one like a son of man, and he came to the Ancient of Days and was presented before him. And to him was given dominion and glory and a kingdom, that all peoples, nations, and languages should serve him; his dominion is an everlasting dominion, which shall not pass away, and his kingdom is one that shall not be destroyed.*
>
> —Daniel 7:13–14

- How does this passage describe the kingdom that is received from the Ancient of Days? What sort of people make up this kingdom? How long does it last?

During the Video

▶ *Play the video; pause at 6:23.*

Our Motives for Missions

- What should be our first and foremost motivation for missions?
- What motivation for missions did Christ give His disciples in the Great Commission?
- In what sense does Christ offer His disciples words of comfort in the Great Commission?

▶ *Play the video; pause at 13:41.*

Authority over All

- Why is the recurring use of the word "all" in the Great Commission significant?
- How did Jesus respond to the temptation of the devil for all the kingdoms of the earth? What does His response tell you about the type of the authority that belonged to Satan?
- In the Great Commission, Jesus proclaimed, "All authority in heaven and on earth has been given to me." What is the basic inference of the last words of this statement?

After the Video

- How are the words of comfort and assurance with which Christ approached His disciples in the Great Commission significant for us?

  If you are in a group, have the members recount some times when they have had the opportunity to evangelize someone, particularly focusing on ways that God uniquely equipped them for the situation.

- What was Dr. Parsons' fundamental argument about the compatibility of things such as prayer, evangelism, and missions with the sovereignty of God?

If you are in a group, have the members discuss how they came to accept the truths of Calvinism and Reformed theology and to what degree they wrestled—or still wrestle—with the doctrines of grace.

- Should the doctrine of election motivate us to take part in God's mission? Why or why not? How does the doctrine of election determine to whom we proclaim the gospel?

If you are in a group, have each member identify a moment in the life of Jesus Christ that has had the most impact on them as a display of Christ's willingness to serve others—for instance, the way He served His closest companions or how he reached out to the outcasts of society.

PRAYER

- Praise God for His sovereign power and authority.
- Confess the areas in your life where you have been reluctant to trust God.
- Thank God for teaching you how even the disciples needed words of assurance.
- Ask God to reassure you through and deepen your appreciation of the doctrines of grace.

REVIEW QUIZ

1. What motivation for missions is found in the first line of the Great Commission?
   a. Love of God
   b. Love of neighbor
   c. Sovereignty of God
   d. Obedience to Christ

2. Which of the following words best describes the sovereignty of Jesus Christ?
   a. Limited
   b. Spiritual
   c. Universal
   d. Contingent

3. What is a key word in the Great Commission for recognizing the extent of Christ's rule?
   a. Authority
   b. Disciples
   c. Nations
   d. All

4. What rhetorical device is used in the Great Commission to qualify Christ's authority?
   a. Merism
   b. Hendiadys
   c. Hyperbole
   d. Synecdoche

5. A common assumption is that the sovereignty of God contradicts our need to evangelize.
   a. True
   b. False

6. Which of the following best summarizes why evangelism and missions are difficult?
   a. Evangelism and missions entail knowing who the elect of God are.
   b. Evangelism and missions succeed by the work of the Holy Spirit.
   c. Evangelism and missions require telling people hard truths.
   d. Evangelism and missions rest on the sovereignty of God.

Answer Key—All Authority in Heaven and on Earth

REFLECTION & DISCUSSION QUESTIONS

Before the Video

What Do You Think?

These are personal questions. The answers should be based on your own knowledge and experience.

Scripture Reading

- How does this passage describe the kingdom that is received from the Ancient of Days? What sort of people make up this kingdom? How long does it last?

  This passage describes a kingdom that will be made up of people from all nations and languages, who are to serve the "one like a son of man," who we know to be Jesus Christ. His kingdom is an everlasting kingdom "that shall not be destroyed."

During the Video

Our Motives for Missions

- What should be our first and foremost motivation for missions?

  Our first and foremost motivation for missions should be the love of God, which is the first and great commandment of the law: "You shall love the Lord your God with all your heart and with all your soul and with all your mind" (Matt. 22:37).

- What motivation for missions did Christ give His disciples in the Great Commission?

  The first words of the Great Commission are, "All authority in heaven and on earth has been given to me." With these words, Christ gave His disciples a significant and powerful motivation for missions: Christ's own sovereignty over the nations.

- In what sense does Christ offer His disciples words of comfort in the Great Commission?

  In the introductory lesson of this series, we learned how some of the disciples doubted and were perhaps fearful upon seeing Christ from a distance. When Christ approached them, He did not rebuke them or remind them of their faithlessness and failures. What may appear to us, at first glance, to be merely words about Christ's sovereign authority are actually words of great comfort and assurance to a band of fearful disciples who were trembling in the presence of God.

Authority over All

- Why is the reoccurring use of the word "all" in the Great Commission of significance?

  The word "all" appears multiple times in the Great Commission. Christ has "all" rule and authority. The disciples are to go into "all" nations to teach them "all" that Christ has commanded. As the disciples carry out this mission, Christ promised to be with them "always." The use of the word "all" in the Great Commission points to the universal aspect of Christ's rule and reign.

- How did Jesus respond to the temptation of the devil for all the kingdoms of the earth? What does His response tell you about the type of the authority that belonged to Satan?

  Jesus responded to the devil's temptation by quoting Scripture: "You shall worship the Lord your God, and him only shall you serve" (Matt. 4:10; see Deut. 6:13). Jesus' response points us to the highest authority, which tells us that Satan's authority can only be described as limited—nothing in comparison with God's authority.

- In the Great Commission, Jesus proclaimed, "All authority in heaven and on earth has been given to me." What is the basic inference of the last words of this statement?

  The last words of this statement reveal that Christ received His authority from someone. The basic inference is that Christ received His sovereign authority from no one else but His sovereign and almighty Father.

After the Video

- How are the words of comfort and assurance with which Christ approached His disciples in the Great Commission significant for us?

  Christ's words to His disciples are significant for us because we also need these words of comfort and assurance. Like the disciples, we may not feel like conquerors but rather like failures, so we need Christ's words of assurance for the hard work of missions and evangelism, which involves telling people hard truths. Let us be encouraged by Christ's words and trust in His sovereign Spirit to equip us for His work.

- What was Dr. Parsons' fundamental argument about the compatibility of things such as prayer, evangelism, and missions with the sovereignty of God?

  Dr. Parsons argued that things such as prayer, evangelism, and missions would not even be possible without the sovereignty of God because the sovereignty of God is central to our own salvation. Apart from God's sovereignty, we would be still dead in our trespasses and sins, let alone able to pray, evangelize, or play a role in God's mission.

- Should the doctrine of election motivate us to take part in God's mission? Why or why not? How does the doctrine of election determine to whom we proclaim the gospel?

  The doctrine of election should motivate us to take part in God's mission because it assures us that our work will be fruitful on the basis of God's will to save His elect. Because we know that God has elected some to salvation but we do not know whom He has elected, we go to every tribe, tongue, and nation and preach to all regardless of their ancestry, background, color, or socioeconomic class. We go to the ends of the earth for the sake of God's elect.

REVIEW QUIZ

1. **C.**
   The sovereignty of God is the primary motivation for missions found in the opening line of the Great Commission: "All authority in heaven and on earth has been given to me." In this lecture, Dr. Parsons mentioned both our love of God and our love for our neighbor as motives for missions, but these are not explicit in the Great Commission's opening line.

2. **C.**
   By definition, sovereignty isn't limited or dependent on anything else or merely spiritual. Christ's sovereignty is then best described as universal. This is the word Dr. Parsons used to emphasize the all-encompassing aspect of Christ's sovereignty.

3. **D.**
   In the Great Commission, the word "all" is a key to help us recognize the true extent of Christ's rule. Depending on the translation, "all" can appear three or four times, demonstrating in various ways how Christ's authority extends over all for all time.

4. **A.**
   The rhetorical device used in the Great Commission to qualify Christ's authority is called a merism, which is when two contrasting words are used to express an entirety. Christ has been given all authority "in heaven and on earth," meaning that there is no place where Christ's authority does not extend. We also see a merism in Genesis 1:1, where God created "the heavens and the earth."

5. **A.**
   It is a false assumption, but it is true that people typically assume that the idea of God's sovereignty contradicts our need to pray or evangelize. This objection against the sovereignty of God fails to recognize that, apart from Him, we would all be dead in our trespasses and sins, unable to pray or evangelize in the first place.

6. **C.**
   Evangelism and missions ultimately require sacrifice, and sometimes sacrifice means putting ourselves aside so that we can tell people the hard truths about their sin. We can be confident, even though we don't always feel confident in ourselves, that God is sovereignly at work through His Spirit when we faithfully proclaim the good news of Jesus Christ to all.

3

Go Therefore and Make Disciples of All Nations

INTRODUCTION

The great commandment of the Great Commission is the clear directive of Jesus Christ to "go therefore and make disciples of all nations." This is a command requiring nothing short of our obedience, for it is by going and making disciples that we fulfill the Great Commission. In this lesson, Dr. Parsons teaches us exactly what it means—and what it does not mean—to be and to make disciples of our Lord Jesus Christ.

LEARNING GOALS

When you have finished this lesson, you should be able to:

- Identify another motivation for fulfilling the Great Commission
- Understand the grammar and syntax within the Great Commission
- Discern the difference between true discipleship and false discipleship

KEY IDEAS

- We strive to fulfill the Great Commission out of obedience to Christ.
- Making disciples—not merely making coverts—is how we fulfill the Great Commission.
- Disciples of Jesus Christ are marked by a love for worship, by a love for one another, and by the fruit of obedience and baptism.

REFLECTION & DISCUSSION QUESTIONS

Before the Video

What Do You Think?

- How do you know that you are a disciple of Jesus Christ?
- Has anyone ever taken the time to personally teach you about the ways of the Christian faith? What impact has this had on you as a Christian?

Scripture Reading

> *By this we know that we have come to know him, if we keep his commandments. Whoever says "I know him" but does not keep his commandments is a liar, and the truth is not in him, but whoever keeps his word, in him truly the love of God is perfected.*
>
> —1 John 2:3–5

- What does this passage teach us about someone who knows Jesus Christ? What are the implications of this passage for the Great Commission? Is obedience to the Great Commission optional?

During the Video

Play the video; pause at 4:18.

Obedience to Christ

- Why is Matthew 28:18–20 traditionally called "the Great Commission" and not "the Great Suggestion" or "the Great Option"?
- What is the difference between Christ's authority and the authority of the eleven disciples who received the Great Commission?
- How does the fact that we are under Christ's authority shape our mentality as we go to make disciples?

Play the video; pause at 13:04.

True Disciple Making

- Why should our obedience to the Great Commission extend to reached and unreached people groups?
- What mistake can be made by churches and missions organizations without a careful study of the Great Commission?
- What did the earthly ministry of Jesus Christ look like in terms of discipleship? What does this demonstrate about the work of discipleship?

After the Video

- What might a person's infrequency in attending or avoidance of congregational worship indicate?

If you are in a group, have the members share how their attitude toward worship changed after they had become a Christian.

- What does true discipleship look like? What type of disciple does it produce? How does such a disciple relate to the doctrines of the faith?

  If you are in a group, have the members share stories about meaningful encounters when they were discipled by or discipled another Christian. How formative were these experiences for their faith or the faith of another?

- What is significant about where the Great Commission mentions baptism? In light of the requirements of the Great Commission, how are Christians to disciple their children?

  If you are in a group, have the members discuss their understanding and view of infant baptism. Do you agree with Dr. Parsons? If so, why? If not, how do you respond to the arguments he made for infant baptism in this lecture?

PRAYER

- Praise God for His desire to have disciples from every tribe, tongue, and nation.
- Confess any lack of effort in pursuing relationships where you can disciple others.
- Thank God for the people in your life who have played a major role in your discipleship.
- Ask God to give you a passion for discipleship, both to train and also to learn from others.

REVIEW QUIZ

1. In this lesson, what is the sufficient motivation for fulfilling the Great Commission?
   a. Love of God
   b. Love of neighbor
   c. Sovereignty of God
   d. Obedience to Christ

2. What word describes the type of authority exercised by a minister of the Word?
   a. Free
   b. Inherent
   c. Declarative
   d. Absolute

3. Which of the following statements is true about baptism?
   a. Baptism is not a part of discipleship.
   b. Baptism is a graduating rite.
   c. Baptism regenerates a person.
   d. Baptism is an initiating rite.

4. What is the prominent verb that controls the entirety of the Great Commission?
   a. Go
   b. Make disciples
   c. Baptizing
   d. Teaching

5. Making converts to the faith in itself fulfills the Great Commission.
   a. True
   b. False

6. Which of the following is true about the grammar and syntax of the Great Commission?
   a. There are three subordinate clauses modifying "make disciples."
   b. The verb "go" is a participle in the Greek but is best translated as an imperative.
   c. The verb "go" is an imperative in the Greek and is translated that way in English.
   d. The idea of baptism is introduced within the second subordinate clause modifying "make disciples."

Answer Key—Go Therefore and Make Disciples of All Nations

REFLECTION & DISCUSSION QUESTIONS

Before the Video

What Do You Think?

These are personal questions. The answers should be based on your own knowledge and experience.

Scripture Reading

- What does this passage teach us about someone who knows Jesus Christ? What are the implications of this passage for the Great Commission? Is obedience to the Great Commission optional?

  This passage teaches us that one who knows Jesus Christ will keep His commandments, and in such a person the love of God is perfected. In relation to the Great Commission, we must recognize that it is a command from our Lord Jesus Christ, so obedience to it demonstrates that we know Christ. If it is a command, it isn't an option.

During the Video

Obedience to Christ

- Why is Matthew 28:18–20 traditionally called "the Great Commission" and not "the Great Suggestion" or "the Great Option"?

  A commission is a command, so Matthew 28:18–20 has traditionally been called "the Great Commission" because it is a command from our Lord Jesus Christ, which alone should be sufficient motivation for our taking part in its fulfillment.

- What is the difference between Christ's authority and the authority of the eleven disciples who received the Great Commission?

  Christ has authority in and of Himself as Lord over all. In contrast, the eleven disciples did not have any inherent authority but were commissioned to go forth in His authority. This is analogous to the declarative authority of an ordained minister of the gospel.

- How does the fact that we are under Christ's authority shape our mentality as we go to make disciples?

  As those under authority, we do not undertake missions on our own authority, seeking to gain applause for our endeavors. Rather, we set out with a mentality of meekness as humble servants of Jesus Christ. The fact that we are under

His authority ought to humble us and enables us to point others to Him and not ourselves.

True Disciple Making

- Why should our obedience to the Great Commission extend to reached and unreached people groups?

  Obedience to the Great Commission means that we will go to all people, both reached and unreached people groups. This is because discipleship is an integral part of the Great Commission. Our obedience should extend to unreached people groups so that they might hear and believe, but it should also continue to extend to reached people groups so that they might mature in their knowledge of our Lord.

- What mistake can be made by churches and missions organizations without a careful study of the Great Commission?

  Without a careful study of all that the Great Commission entails, churches and missions organizations may think that the Great Commission is being fulfilled through evangelism or Bible translation. While these activities are very important in fulfilling the Great Commission, it is a mistake to think that the Great Commission is only about evangelism or making converts when discipleship is not taking place.

- What did the earthly ministry of Jesus Christ look like in terms of discipleship? What does this demonstrate about the work of discipleship?

  During His earthly ministry, Jesus trained men peripatetically, that is, He allowed men to follow Him, learn from His teaching, and observe the way He interacted with others. This demonstrates how the work of discipleship takes considerable time and effort and involves training on an intimate and personal level.

After the Video

- What might a person's infrequency in attending or avoidance of congregational worship indicate?

  At best, infrequency in attending or avoidance of congregational worship on the Lord's Day might be indicative of disobedience to the Great Commission, as worship is one of the ways in which we fulfill it. At worst, it might be indicative of a lack of faith—that a person has never been reached by the good news of the gospel in the first place.

- What does true discipleship look like? What type of disciple does it produce? How does such a disciple relate to the doctrines of the faith?

  True discipleship involves personal training in the faith, which takes time and hard work but bears good fruit for God's glory. This is because a true disciple seeks to be obedient to all that Christ commands, bearing fruit in repentance and loving and forgiving others. Such a disciple loves to worship God and carefully studies the doctrines of the faith, not just to know them, but to apply them through good works.

- What is significant about where the Great Commission mentions baptism? In light of the requirements of the Great Commission, how are Christians to disciple their children?

  The command to make disciples has two subordinating clauses that teach us how we are to make disciples. The first clause indicates that part of the way we make disciples is through baptizing them. Baptism is mentioned first in the Great Commission, showing us that baptism is an initiating rite, not a graduating rite. It is administered to those who are being initiated into the covenant community. In light of the emphasis on discipleship in the Great Commission, Christians are to disciple their children through baptizing them and teaching them the things of God. We are to teach our children how to sing, worship, pray, and read the Bible and teach them what it is to know God through saving faith in Jesus Christ.

REVIEW QUIZ

1. **D.**

   In this lecture, Dr. Parsons focused on obedience to Christ as another motivation for missions. Obedience to Christ can be called the sufficient motivation for missions due to the fact that it alone is reason enough to take our part in the Great Commission, for it is a command from our Lord.

2. **C.**

   Ministers of the Word of God do not have any authority in and of themselves. Their authority is declarative or ministerial. They have authority to declare the Word of God. This is unlike Christ's authority over heaven and earth, which is inherent and absolute.

3. **D.**

   Baptism is one of the first steps in becoming a disciple of Christ and is an initiating rite of the faith. It is not something we must work up to in order to be welcomed into the covenant community. Baptism also does not save or regenerate; regeneration is the work of the Holy Spirit alone in giving us the ability to savingly trust in Jesus Christ.

4. **B.**

   The verb that governs the entirety of the Great Commission is Christ's imperative to make disciples. It is the purpose for going to all the nations, and even on a grammatical level, "baptizing" and "teaching" both mark subordinate participial clauses.

5. **B.**

   Making converts is only a part of what it means to fulfill the Great Commission, for we can make converts without making disciples. The Great Commission is not being fulfilled unless we are making disciples according to how disciples are defined in the New Testament.

6. **B.**

   The verb "go" is actually a participle in the Greek, but due to the way it is constructed in the sentence it is rightly translated in the form of an imperative, as a command. In the Great Commission, there are only two subordinate participial clauses, and baptism is introduced in the first.

4

Teaching Them to Observe All I Have Commanded

INTRODUCTION

In making disciples of all nations, what exactly are we to teach? Are we to share our testimonies? Tell people about specific events and teachings in the life of Jesus Christ? What about the rest of the Bible? In this lesson, Dr. Parsons focuses on the content of what we are to teach people in order that they might know what it is to faithfully follow Christ, who is the fulfillment of all of Scripture.

LEARNING GOALS

When you have finished this lesson, you should be able to:

- Trace God's heart for the nations from the Old Testament to the New Testament
- Recognize the pivotal importance of teaching in making disciples of Christ
- Summarize all that Christ has called us to observe in the Great Commission

KEY IDEAS

- In the Great Commission, we take our part in God's original promise to Abraham to bless all the families of the earth, a promise ultimately fulfilled in Christ.
- Obedience is a foundational, commonly overlooked concept in the Great Commission.
- Faithfulness to the Great Commission requires teaching others to obey all of Scripture.

REFLECTION & DISCUSSION QUESTIONS

Before the Video

What Do You Think?

- What is the gospel?
- Is it safe to assume that the average person on the street has never heard the gospel? What would someone have to know in order to understand what it is to be a Christian?

Scripture Reading

> *Now the LORD said to Abram, "Go from your country and your kindred and your father's house to the land that I will show you. And I will make you a great nation, and I will bless you and make your name great, so that you will be a blessing. I will bless those who bless you, and him who dishonors you I will curse, and in you all the families of the earth shall be blessed." So Abram went, as the LORD had told him.*
>
> —Genesis 12:1–4a

- What are some similarities between the call of Abraham and the Great Commission?

During the Video

Play the video; pause at 7:50.

Abraham's Calling, Our Calling

- What type of person was Abraham before he was called by God? Why is this significant?
- Relative to Abraham, why is the genealogy that begins the gospel of Matthew important?
- How does the Great Commission connect us to God's promise to Abraham?

Play the video; pause at 15:00.

The Importance of Teaching

- In the previous lesson, we learned about the importance of baptism for making disciples. What else is necessary for making disciples according to the Great Commission?
- What does the phrase "shepherds and teachers" reveal about the duties of a pastor?
- According to James 3:1, why should there not be many teachers? What are some of the implications of this for people pursuing vocational ministry? Does it mean that there is a standard of truth contained in the Bible?

After the Video

- What is the first thing that we need for faithfulness to the Great Commission?

  If you are in a group, have the members name the various ways in which the Holy Spirit works to secure our salvation. In what ways is the Spirit at work for us before, during, and after we became Christians?

- Are all Christians called to be teachers or only some Christians? Likewise, are all Christians called to participate in God's mission or only some Christians?

  If you are in a group, have the members talk about the various opportunities in their lives where they are able to teach someone about the Christian faith. Pray that these would bear fruit by the power of the Spirit.

- What important part of the Great Commission is often forgotten or overlooked? In what way is this part of the Great Commission fundamental for true discipleship?

  If you are in a group, have the members discuss what nuances of the word "observe" they consider to be the most forceful in conveying how we are to uphold all that Christ has commanded us and why.

PRAYER

- Praise God for His ability to use even fallen men to teach His spotless Word.
- Confess sins in which you have knowingly failed to observe all that Christ has commanded.
- Thank God for the work of the Holy Spirit in sustaining you as a disciple of Jesus Christ.
- Ask God to grant you deeper knowledge of His Word so that you might live for His glory.

REVIEW QUIZ

1. What is safe to assume about the reach of the gospel to foreigners or even to average citizens in the United States?
   a. They've heard the gospel of Jesus Christ.
   b. They've never heard the gospel of Jesus Christ.
   c. They've embraced the gospel but live contrary to it.
   d. They've never embraced the gospel due to a rational dilemma.

2. With whom does Matthew's genealogy begin?
   a. Joseph
   b. David
   c. Abraham
   d. Adam

3. In which gospel is there a parallel account of the Great Commission that teaches us about our need to be empowered by the Holy Spirit for missions?
   a. Matthew
   b. Mark
   c. Luke
   d. John
4. The phrase "shepherds and teachers" uses a rhetorical device that uses two words to refer to one thing. What is this device called?
   a. Merism
   b. Hyperbole
   c. Hendiadys
   d. Synecdoche
5. Where there is a church, the gospel is proclaimed.
   a. True
   b. False
6. Which of the following is *not* a nuance of "to observe" in the Great Commission?
   a. To guard
   b. To keep
   c. To obey
   d. To learn

Answer Key—Teaching Them to Observe All I Have Commanded

REFLECTION & DISCUSSION QUESTIONS

Before the Video

What Do You Think?

These are personal questions. The answers should be based on your own knowledge and experience.

Scripture Reading

- What are some similarities between the call of Abraham and the Great Commission?

  The first similarity is found with the command to "go." The second similarity can be found in the fact that the nations are the object of blessing through the faithfulness of Abraham and the disciples. Let us pray that a third similarity may be found in us, that we would be obedient to the call as Abraham was.

During the Video

Abraham's Calling, Our Calling

- What type of person was Abraham before he was called by God? Why is this significant?

  Before being called, Abraham was a rebellious enemy of God. He was a pagan from Ur of the Chaldeans. He was not seeking after God, nor was he concerned with the things of God. This is significant because it demonstrates how God is the One who initiated a relationship with Abraham. God is the One who first reaches out and saves.

- Relative to Abraham, why is the genealogy that begins the gospel of Matthew important?

  The gospel of Matthew begins with a genealogy that masterfully connects the life of Jesus with the life of Abraham. By doing this, Matthew displays how Jesus is the long-awaited Messiah from the seed of Abraham and how Jesus is the fulfillment of the Abrahamic covenant, the true and greater Abraham through whom the nations will be reached.

- How does the Great Commission connect us to God's promise to Abraham?

  God promised that all the families of the earth would be blessed through Abraham. This promise has been realized in Christ, but it continues through our obedience to the Great Commission. As Christians, we have received the blessing of God's promise to Abraham, yet we are also sent out and used for the further fulfillment of God's promise. Through our faithfulness to the Great Commission, we take part in God's original promise to Abraham to bless all the families of the earth.

The Importance of Teaching

- In the previous lesson, we learned about the importance of baptism for making disciples. What else is necessary for making disciples according to the Great Commission?

  The Great Commission makes clear that teaching is necessary for making disciples of Christ. "Teaching them to observe" begins the second subordinate clause that describes what it means to make disciples of the nations. Teaching is one of the ways in which we bring the true light of the gospel of God to a dark world.

- What does the phrase "shepherds and teachers" reveal about the duties of a pastor?

  The phrase "shepherds and teachers" is used by Paul in Ephesian 4 to describe in two titles the one church office of pastor. Pastors are called to both shepherd and teach the people of God. Through their work as shepherds, pastors guide, counsel, administer the sacraments, administer discipline, serve, and pray. Through their work as teachers, they preach and teach the Word of God to instruct God's people.

- According to James 3:1, why should there not be many teachers? What are some of the implications of this for people pursuing vocational ministry? Does it mean that there is a standard of truth contained in the Bible?

  According to James 3:1, there should not be many teachers because teachers will be held to a higher account and judged with greater strictness. Dr. Parsons discussed some of the implications of this for people pursuing vocational ministry, that they should not just aim for a degree but study to show themselves approved. The notion of a stricter judgment implies that there is a standard of truth by which people can be judged.

After the Video

- What is the first thing that we need for faithfulness to the Great Commission?

  The first thing we need for faithfulness to the Great Commission is the empowerment of the Holy Spirit. This is clearly seen in Luke's parallel account of the Great Commission where Jesus told His disciples to stay in Jerusalem until they were "clothed with power from on high" (Luke 24:49). The Spirit gives us the motivation to go and does all the work to enable us to go, and as we go He saves people through His power.

- Are all Christians called to be teachers or only some Christians? Likewise, are all Christians called to participate in God's mission or only some Christians?

In one sense, not all Christians are equipped to teach in the capacity of an elder, but in another sense, all Christians are involved in teaching in various ways. It may be a mother teaching her child or one Christian teaching another in a Bible study or through a mentoring relationship. Likewise, not all Christians are called into foreign missions, but God does call every Christian to participate in His mission wherever they are.

- What important part of the Great Commission is often forgotten or overlooked? In what way is this part of the Great Commission fundamental for true discipleship?

  The phrase "to observe" is often forgotten or overlooked when people consider the Great Commission. This is a fundamental part of the Great Commission for true discipleship because disciples are not merely filled with head knowledge but are obedient to all the truths of the faith.

REVIEW QUIZ

1. **B.**
   Today, we have to consider that the nations are all around us, which means that, even and especially in America, there are foreigners who have never heard the gospel. This is also true of those who have grown up in America and perhaps have even attended church.

2. **C.**
   Matthew's gospel begins with a genealogy running from Abraham to Jesus Christ. Matthew did this to demonstrate that Jesus is the long-awaited Messiah, the promised seed of Abraham, who has fulfilled God's covenant with Abraham.

3. **C.**
   Luke's account of the Great Commission is where we find Jesus telling His disciples to wait in Jerusalem for "power from on high" before setting off to carry the gospel to the ends of the earth (Luke 24:49). From this, we can see our need for the Holy Spirit in missions. The Holy Spirit is mentioned in John's account as well, but not in the context in which Dr. Parsons applied it to the Spirit's empowerment, which took place at Pentecost.

4. **C.**
   Hendiadys is the use of two words in conjunction to refer to a single thing. In the case of "shepherds and teachers," these two words refer to a single church office, so the phrase highlights the different duties of a pastor.

5. **B.**
   The sad truth, in an American context, is that just because there is a church on every corner does not mean that the gospel is proclaimed on every corner. This is why we need to understand that missions isn't only about going to unreached people groups in foreign lands. It is about going to unreached people everywhere, even next door.

6. **D.**

The verb "to observe" has multiple nuances in the Greek: to obey, to keep, and to guard. Dr. Parsons particularly emphasized "to guard" as a nuance of this verb. "To learn" was not listed as a nuance of "to observe," and a distinction was made in this lecture between merely learning and observing all that Christ has commanded.

5

I Am with You Always

INTRODUCTION

The Great Commission ends with the comforting words "I am with you always, to the end of the age." While comforting, these words can be perplexing, causing us to ask, "How is Christ with us to the end of the age?" In this lesson, Dr. Parsons answers this question through a sketch of one of the most significant themes in all of Scripture, revealing God's enduring desire to dwell with His people and even to use us to fulfill His mission through the local church.

LEARNING GOALS

When you have finished this lesson, you should be able to:

- Describe the ways in which God has made His dwelling among us
- Discuss the significance of the Holy Spirit in the work of the Great Commission
- Grasp the importance of the ordinary local church in fulfilling the mission of God

KEY IDEAS

- God dwelling among His people is one of the most significant themes in Scripture.
- Jesus fulfills His promise to be with us through the indwelling of the Holy Spirit.
- "To the end of the age" refers to the culmination of all things upon Christ's return.
- The local church is the primary means through which the Great Commission is fulfilled.

REFLECTION & DISCUSSION QUESTIONS

Before the Video

What Do You Think?

- Would you do anything to take care of the ones you love? How far would you go to help them and protect them from harm?
- Do you longingly desire the return of Jesus Christ? Why?

Scripture Reading

> *If you love me, you will keep my commandments. And I will ask the Father, and he will give you another Helper, to be with you forever, even the Spirit of truth, whom the world cannot receive, because it neither sees him nor knows him. You know him, for he dwells with you and will be in you. . . . It is to your advantage that I go away, for if I do not go away, the Helper will not come to you. But if I go, I will send him to you.*
>
> —John 14:15–17; 16:7b

- Why is it to our advantage that Jesus has ascended to His Father in heaven? In what ways does Jesus describe the Holy Spirit?

During the Video

Play the video; pause at 12:46.

God with Us

- How does the Great Commission begin and end with words of comfort and reassurance?
- God dwelling among His people is one of the great themes of the Bible. What then is the significance of Jesus' telling His disciples that He would be with them always?
- Why does the Holy Spirit receive all the glory in the Great Commission's fulfillment?

Play the video to the end.

The Fulfillment of the Great Commission

- How is the phrase "to the end of the age" best understood?
- What is a good reason to pursue full-time vocational ministry?
- In what way is the local church central to the fulfillment of the Great Commission?

After the Video

- How is God's intimate relationship with man revealed in the creation of Adam and in the garden of Eden with Adam and Eve?

If you are in a group, have the members name some of the many examples given by Dr. Parsons of how God has made Himself present with His people throughout Scripture. Have the members discuss their favorite example and say why it is their favorite.

- How does the sovereign work of the Holy Spirit inform the way we are to go about the work of missions and preaching and teaching?

  If you are in a group, have the members talk about some of the strategies that they have encountered in churches that seem to depart from the ordinary means that God uses to save people. Feel free also to use examples from church history.

- What is the most important concept you have learned in studying the Great Commission?

  If you are in a group, have each member identify the most important concept they have learned in this teaching series and discuss the significance of these concepts.

PRAYER

- Praise God for His enduring desire to be with His people and to make Himself known to them.
- Confess ways in which you have grieved the Spirit by sinning against fellow Christians.
- Thank God for indwelling you by the Holy Spirit, for giving you nothing short of Himself.
- Ask God to use you as a vital part of your local church in fulfilling the Great Commission.

REVIEW QUIZ

1. What attribute of God was emphasized in this lecture as a source of our comfort?
   a. God's omnipotence
   b. God's omnipresence
   c. God's transcendence
   d. God's immanence

2. Where can you find an outline of the ordinary work of the early church in Scripture?
   a. John 3
   b. Acts 2
   c. Romans 9
   d. Ephesians 4

3. Relative to the central theme of this lecture, why is it better that Jesus return to His Father than be physically present with us?
   a. To return to the glory He shared with the Father
   b. To receive the highest authority from the Father
   c. To intercede for us when we pray to the Father
   d. To send the Holy Spirit after asking the Father
4. For whom is reserved a great passion for the Great Commission?
   a. Pastors
   b. Scholars
   c. Christians
   d. Missionaries
5. We should associate the phrase "to the end of the age" with something like the ending of a book or the ending of a movie.
   a. True
   b. False
6. What is the primary means God has given for the advancement of the Great Commission?
   a. The proper administration of the sacraments
   b. The preaching of the Word
   c. The study of Scripture
   d. The local church

Answer Key—I Am with You Always

REFLECTION & DISCUSSION QUESTIONS

Before the Video

What Do You Think?

These are personal questions. The answers should be based on your own knowledge and experience.

Scripture Reading

- Why is it to our advantage that Jesus has ascended to His Father in heaven? In what ways does Jesus describe the Holy Spirit?

  It is to our advantage that Jesus has ascended to His Father in heaven because it is from there that He sends to us the Helper, the promised Holy Spirit. Jesus describes the Holy Spirit as "another Helper," a phrase that is commonly used in support of the divinity of the Holy Spirit. Additionally, we can see that the Holy Spirit will be with us forever as the Spirit of truth, whom we have received and who indwells us to the end of the age.

During the Video

God with Us

- How does the Great Commission begin and end with words of comfort and reassurance?

  Jesus begins the Great Commission by comforting and reassuring His trembling disciples that all authority in heaven and on earth have been given to Him; this is the foundation for His command to go and make disciples. Jesus further reassures them that He would be with them to the end of the age, ending the Great Commission on the same comforting note that it began.

- God dwelling among His people is one of the great themes of the Bible. What then is the significance of Jesus' telling His disciples that He would be with them always?

  With the words "I am with you always," Jesus is assuring His disciples that He is the fulfillment of Old Testament prophecy. He is Immanuel—God with us—the promised incarnation of the Son of God (Isa. 7:14; Matt. 1:23).

- Why does the Holy Spirit receive all the glory in the Great Commission's fulfillment?

  The Holy Spirit receives all the glory in the Great Commission's fulfillment because it is the Holy Spirit who goes before us, preparing hearts and minds and awakening them with the truth of the gospel. The Holy Spirit truly does the work of indwelling us, uniting us to Christ, and empowering us as secondary agents of God's sovereign providence—never once allowing the mission of God to be thwarted.

The Fulfillment of the Great Commission

- How is the phrase "to the end of the age" best understood?

  The phrase "to the end of the age" is best understood not in terms of the end of the world but in terms of the final consummation of all things. The end of the age is marked by the return of Christ, who will usher in the new heavens and new earth, renovating the world as we know it, not bringing it to its full and final end.

- What is a good reason to pursue full-time vocational ministry?

  A good reason to go into full-time vocational ministry is a deep, urgent passion to see the Great Commission fulfilled. People who are called to ministry recognize that the mission of God is the most important thing they could ever be a part of and desire to give their lives to it. That being said, it is important to remember that God's mission isn't limited, because every Christian is called to be passionately involved in it for His glory.

- In what way is the local church central to the fulfillment of the Great Commission?

  The local church is where every aspect of the Great Commission is carried out. It is in the local church that disciples are made, the sacraments are administered, and the gospel goes forth through the preaching of the Word. Missions itself takes places within the context of a church as the church sends in order to make more disciples and establish more churches.

After the Video

- How is God's intimate relationship with man revealed in the creation of Adam and in the garden of Eden with Adam and Eve?

  God did not create Adam from a distance. Rather, in the creation of man, we have a close and intimate portrait of Almighty God condescending and breathing into man's nostrils the breath of life. In the garden of Eden, God was likewise intimately close with Adam and Eve, walking with them in the cool of the day (Gen. 3:8).

- How does the sovereign work of the Holy Spirit inform the way we are to go about the work of missions and preaching and teaching?

  The sovereign work of the Holy Spirit informs us that our work in missions and preaching and teaching does not have to employ manipulative tactics and schemes to achieve what only the Holy Spirit can do. The Holy Spirit uses the unadorned Word of God to achieve His sovereign purposes in salvation, a fact that our work in missions and preaching and teaching should reflect.

- What is the most important concept you have learned in studying the Great Commission?

The answer to this question should express what you considered the most important concept you learned while studying the Great Commission.

REVIEW QUIZ

1. **D.**
   In this lecture, Dr. Parsons emphasized how the last words in the Great Commission are words of comfort because in them Jesus promised to be with us always. This is tied to God's attribute of immanence, His nearness to His creatures and to His creation. All of God's attributes are a comfort to His people, but God's immanence is strongly accented in Christ's promise and the fulfillment of it through the indwelling Spirit.

2. **B.**
   In this lecture, Dr. Parsons read from Acts 2:41–47. This passage of Scripture teaches us about the way things were done in the early church, and there we find the elements of a faithful ordinary church, obedient to the Great Commission through the ordinary means of grace.

3. **D.**
   All of the answer choices are true of Christ's session at the right hand of the Father, but in this lecture the central theme has been God's presence with us in the person of the Holy Spirit as promised to us by Christ in the Great Commission. John 16 was quoted in this lecture, where Jesus told His disciples that it was to their advantage that He ascend to the Father so that He could ask for and send the Holy Spirit.

4. **C.**
   A great passion for the Great Commission is for all Christians. It isn't reserved for only pastors, missionaries, or scholars. It is for all those who follow Jesus. A great passion for the Great Commission is certainly necessary for vocational ministry, but it is not reserved for only those in vocational ministry.

5. **B.**
   The phrase "to the end of the age" does not refer to the end of the world as if it were the end of a book or a movie. Rather, the end of the age is the culmination of all things when Christ returns to make the heavens and earth new. The world doesn't end; it is reborn.

6. **D.**
   While each of these are certainly means that God uses to advance His mission, the primary means through which the Great Commission is fulfilled is through the local church, where every aspect of the Great Commission is carried out—where disciples are initiated through baptism and taught obedience through the preaching of the Word.